Color Your Own
PATRIOTIC
POSTERS

Eric Gottesman

DOVER PUBLICATIONS, INC.
Mineola, New York

NOTE

Designed to instill patriotism and confidence as well as to boost morale, war posters of the First and Second World Wars were used to persuade all Americans to contribute in some way to the war effort. Widespread use of the poster during World War I and World War II helped to create such enduring American icons as Uncle Sam and Rosie the Riveter, truly definitive images of the twentieth century. The posters presented here provide just a glimpse of the wartime propaganda that was used by a variety of artists. Included in this collection are posters that promote recruitment, encourage ship building and industrial productivity, and promote food production, conservation, and wartime savings.

All thirty of the vintage posters in this book are shown in full color on the inside front and back covers. Use this color scheme as a guide to create your own version of a patriotic poster or use different colors to see the effects of mood and tone.

Copyright

Copyright © 2003 by Dover Publications, Inc.
All rights reserved.

Bibliographical Note

Color Your Own Patriotic Posters is a new work, first published by Dover Publications, Inc., in 2003.

International Standard Book Number

ISBN-13: 978-0-486-42650-1
ISBN-10: 0-486-42650-5

Manufactured in the United States by Courier Corporation
42650506   2013
www.doverpublications.com

1. World War I poster by Joseph Christian Leyendecker, ca. 1917.

2.   World War I poster by Howard Chandler Christy, 1917.

3.   World War I poster by James Montgomery Flagg, 1917.

4. World War I poster by James Montgomery Flagg, 1917.

5. World War I poster by Harrison Fisher, 1918.

6. World War I poster by Howard Chandler Christy, 1919.

7.   World War I poster by Paul Honoré.

8.   World War I poster by Charles Buckles Falls, 1918.

9.   World War I poster by Joseph Christian Leyendecker, ca. 1918.

10. World War I poster by Walter Whitehead, 1918.

11.   World War I poster by Sidney H. Riesenberg, ca. 1917.

WE CAN DO NO OTHERWISE

"THE SWORD IS DRAWN THE NAVY UPHOLDS IT!"
U.S. NAVY RECRUITING STATION

12. World War I poster by Kenyon Cox.

13. World War I poster by Jessie Willcox Smith, 1918.

14. World War I poster, artist unknown, ca. 1914–1918.

15. World War II poster, artist unknown.

16. World War II poster by J. Walter Wilkinson and Walter G. Wilkinson, 1942.

17.   World War II poster by Anton Otto Fischer, 1942.

18. World War II poster by Alfred Charles Parker, 1942.

19. World War II poster by J. Howard Miller, ca. 1942.

20. World War II poster by Lawrence B. Smith, 1942.

21. World War II poster by Bernard Perlin and David Stone Martin, 1943.

22.   World War II poster by McClelland Barclay, 1941–1942.

23.   World War II poster, Department of Agriculture War Boards, 1943.

24. World War II poster, artist unknown, 1943.

25. World War II poster by Tom Woodburn.

26.   World War II poster by Georges Schreiber, 1943.

27.   World War II poster by Georges Schreiber, 1943.

28.   World War II poster by Jon Whitcomb, 1944.

29. World War II poster by Dean Cornwell, 1945.

30.   World War II poster by C. C. Beall, 1945.